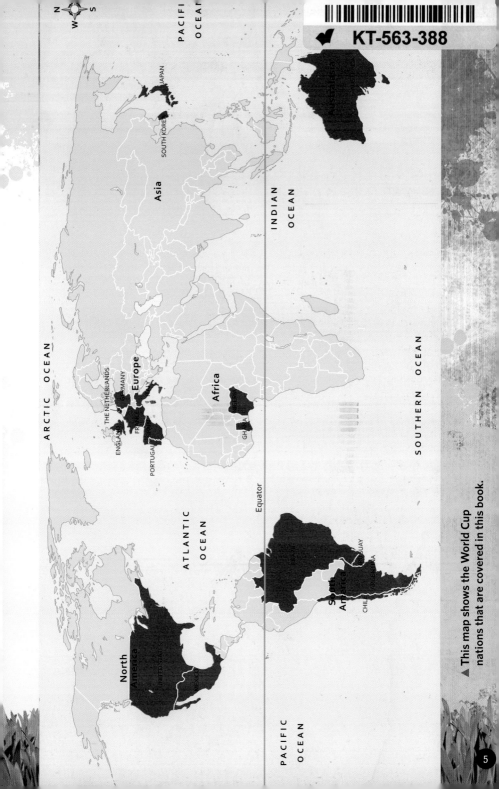

▲ This map shows the World Cup nations that are covered in this book.

5

SOUTH AMERICA

Argentina

CONTINENT: South America
POPULATION: 40.7 million
CAPITAL CITY: Buenos Aires
CURRENCY: peso
LANGUAGE: Spanish
INTERNET: .ar
WORLD CUPS: 15
WORLD CUP WINS: 2 (1978, 1986)
STAR PLAYER: Lionel Messi

PLAYERS TO WATCH:
Ángel di María
Carlos Tevez
Sergio Aguero

FORMER STAR PLAYERS:
Mario Kempes
Diego Maradona
Gabriel Batistuta

TEAM NICKNAME:
La Albiceleste

Argentina has won the World Cup twice, in 1978 and 1986. In 1978 Argentina hosted the World Cup and beat the Netherlands 3–1 in the final. In 1986 Diego Maradona produced some outstanding individual performances, and he led his team all the way to the final and a 3–2 win against West Germany.

ARGENTINA'S GREATEST PLAYER

Maradona is one of the greatest footballers ever to play at the World Cup. His career was full of great moments of skill – but also moments of controversy. At the 1986 World Cup he scored some magnificent goals, including one that is still considered one of the greatest World Cup goals ever. At the same tournament he scored a goal with his hand, but he got away with it. Sadly, in 1994 Maradona was sent home in disgrace from the tournament after testing positive for drugs.

CONTENTS

THE WORLD CUP: NATIONS

When the FIFA World Cup kicks off in Brazil in 2014, there will be 32 football teams representing countries from around the world.

Qualifying to play in the World Cup can be a long, hard road for the teams. There are officially 209 member nations of FIFA. Nations from the same continent compete against each other to qualify to play at the world's most famous and prestigious football tournament.

Just 13 football teams took part in the 1930 inaugural World Cup in Uruguay. The 2014 World Cup will be the 20th edition of the competition, which has grown in terms of the number of teams participating and the number of spectators. Today the tournament is a major international sporting event that is watched by millions of football fans from all around the world.

FAME AND LEGENDS

Some nations have produced football teams whose performances and results at the World Cup have become legendary. Countries such as Brazil (see page 8) and Italy (see page 22) have fantastic records at the World Cup. Many of the individual players who have represented their countries at the World Cup have become famous because of their outstanding performances at the tournament.

There are other nations that have only been represented a few times at the World Cup. However, they have often left their mark on the competition by reaching the final, or producing a surprise result against more experienced opponents.

ARGENTINA'S WORLD CUP RECORD	
PLAYED	70
WON	37
DRAWN	13
LOST	20
FOR	123
AGAINST	180
WIN %	52.85

OTHER SPORTING SUCCESSES

Argentina beat the favourites USA to the basketball gold medal at the 2004 Olympics. Argentina has also won the Olympic football tournament twice, in 2004 and 2008.

FOOTBALL FACTS

Argentina was one of the 13 teams that took part in the inaugural FIFA World Cup in 1930. Argentina reached the final, but lost 4–2 to the host country Uruguay.

Argentina's basketball team celebrate their victory at the 2004 Olympics.

Brazil

CONTINENT: South America
POPULATION: 196.6 million
CAPITAL CITY: Brasilia
CURRENCY: real
LANGUAGE: Portuguese
INTERNET: .br
WORLD CUPS: 19
WORLD CUP WINS: 5 (1958, 1962, 1970, 1994, 2002)
STAR PLAYER: Neymar

PLAYERS TO WATCH:
Ganso
Oscar
Hulk

FORMER STAR PLAYERS:
Garrincha
Pelé
Romario
Ronaldo

TEAM NICKNAME:
Selecao

▲ Brazil's Garrincha (left) in action against England at the 1962 World Cup.

Brazil is the only country that has taken part in every FIFA World Cup and has produced the most successful teams in the history of the tournament. Brazil has won the competition five times and been runner-up on two other occasions, in 1950 and 1998.

FOOTBALL FACTS

Brazil won the first World Cup final to be decided by a penalty shoot-out. In 1994 in the United States, Brazil's match against Italy finished 0–0 after extra time. Brazil won the shoot-out 3–2.

Between 1958 and 1970 Brazil won three out of four World Cups. The two most exceptional Brazilian players were Garrincha and Pelé. Garrincha had incredible dribbling skills and his performances in the 1962 tournament were outstanding. Pelé, with his tremendous goal-scoring ability and all-round talent, scored goals in the 1958 and 1970 finals.

GREAT STRIKERS

Brazil strikers Romario and Ronaldo have received much praise for their goal-scoring skills. In 1994 Romario's goals were crucial for Brazil, and in 2006 Ronaldo became the greatest goalscorer in World Cup history when he netted his 15th goal at the tournament.

▼ Brazil celebrates after winning the World Cup final match against Italy in 1994.

BRAZIL'S WORLD CUP RECORD

PLAYED	97
WON	67
DRAWN	15
LOST	15
FOR	210
AGAINST	88
WIN %	69

Chile

CONTINENT: South America
POPULATION: 17.3 million
CAPITAL CITY: Santiago
CURRENCY: Chilean peso
LANGUAGE: Spanish
INTERNET: .cl
WORLD CUPS: 8
WORLD CUP WINS: 0
STAR PLAYER: Alexis Sanchez

PLAYERS TO WATCH:
Matías Fernández
Humberto Suazo

FORMER STAR PLAYERS:
Iván Zamorano
Marcelo Salas

TEAM NICKNAME:
La Roja

Chile's best finish at a World Cup was at the 1962 tournament. The 1962 World Cup took place in Chile, and the host nation did very well to get to the semi-final. However, they lost by 4–2 to the eventual winners Brazil.

SOUTH AMERICAN QUALIFYING

Chile has only appeared at two World Cups since 1982, playing at the 1998 and 2010 tournaments. It is difficult for South American teams to qualify regularly because the qualifying process is very competitive. There are always at least 10 teams competing against each other in home and away matches. However, only four or five places are up for grabs, so the competition is intense.

Qualifying matches take place all over South America, and teams have to acclimatize to their surroundings depending on where they are playing. For example, the high altitude in Peru can cause shortness of breath and other health problems. Climate and temperature can also vary in the north and south of the continent.

MOST RECENT WORLD CUP APPEARANCE

Chile performed above expectations at the 2010 World Cup in South Africa. The team's exciting brand of attacking football thrilled the fans. Chile advanced from the group stage but lost 3–0 to the stronger Brazilian team in the next round.

National heroes Marcelo Salas (left) and Iván Zamorano starred for Chile at the 1998 World Cup in France.

CHILE'S WORLD CUP RECORD	
PLAYED	29
WON	9
DRAWN	6
LOST	14
FOR	34
AGAINST	45
WIN %	31

Uruguay

CONTINENT: South America
POPULATION: 3.4 million
CAPITAL CITY: Montevideo
CURRENCY: Uruguayan peso
LANGUAGE: Spanish
INTERNET: .uy
WORLD CUPS: 11
WORLD CUP WINS: 2
STAR PLAYER: Luis Suárez

PLAYERS TO WATCH:
Edinson Cavani
Gaston Ramirez

FORMER STAR PLAYERS:
Enzo Francescoli
Sebastien Abreu
Diego Forlan

TEAM NICKNAME:
La Celeste

Uruguay hosted the first ever World Cup in 1930. Twelve teams were invited and competed along with Uruguay to become the first football world champions. Uruguay won the inaugural tournament, beating Argentina 4–2 in an exciting final match.

DID YOU KNOW?

Uruguay won the first two Olympic football titles, in 1924 and 1928.

▲ **Uruguay's Hector Castro battles for the ball with the Argentina goalkeeper during the 1930 World Cup final.**

Uruguay won their second World Cup trophy in Brazil in 1950. Uruguay caused an upset by beating Brazil 2–1 in the final. The match was played in the Maracana Stadium in front of almost 174,000 spectators – a record crowd for a World Cup match.

URUGUAY'S WORLD CUP RECORD	
PLAYED	47
WON	18
DRAWN	12
LOST	17
FOR	76
AGAINST	65
WIN %	38.29

STAR PLAYER AND CONTROVERSIAL MOMENT

The 2010 World Cup was Uruguay's most successful tournament since 1970. They reached the semi-final with the help of one of their star players, Diego Forlan. Forlan had an outstanding World Cup and scored five goals in seven matches. He was named player of the tournament and was awarded with the FIFA Golden Ball for his achievements.

Controversial striker Luis Suárez was sent off in the quarter-final of the 2010 World Cup. He deliberately handled the ball to prevent a goal in Uruguay's match against Ghana (see above, left). The handball led to a penalty, which Ghana failed to score. Suárez celebrated when the penalty was missed, but his behaviour was not greeted well by many football fans.

ASIA AND AUSTRALASIA

Australia

REGION: Australasia
POPULATION: 22.6 million
CAPITAL CITY: Canberra
CURRENCY: Australian dollar
LANGUAGE: English
INTERNET: .au
WORLD CUPS: 3
WORLD CUP WINS: 0
STAR PLAYER: Tim Cahill

PLAYERS TO WATCH:
Mark Schwartzer
Brett Holman

FORMER STAR PLAYERS:
Brett Emerton
Harry Kewell
Mark Viduka

TEAM NICKNAME:
The Socceroos

Australia first qualified for the World Cup in 1974, but failed to qualify again until 2006. They finished second in their group and played Italy in the second round. It was a close match and Italy scored in the last minute to beat Australia 1–0. In 2010 in South Africa, Australia was unlucky not to advance from the group stage. After a thrashing by Germany in their opening match, Australia got a creditable draw against Ghana, and then beat Serbia. Only goal difference prevented the team proceeding to the second round.

OTHER SPORTING SUCCESS

Australians love their sport. As well as football, cricket and rugby are extremely popular. The Australian cricket team has won the Cricket World Cup four times, including three consecutive wins in 1999, 2003, and 2007. Australia has also twice won the Rugby World Cup, in 1991 and 1999.

AUSTRALIA'S WORLD CUP RECORD	
PLAYED	10
WON	2
DRAWN	3
LOST	5
FOR	8
AGAINST	17
WIN %	20

DID YOU KNOW?

Australia holds the record for the biggest win in World Cup history. During the qualifying rounds for the 2002 World Cup, Australia beat American Samoa 31–0!

▶ The Australian women's cricket team has enjoyed great success. Here they are celebrating defeating England in 2012.

New Zealand

REGION: Australasia

POPULATION: 4.4 million

CAPITAL CITY: Auckland

CURRENCY: New Zealand dollar

LANGUAGE: English

INTERNET: .nz

WORLD CUPS: 2

WORLD CUP WINS: 0

STAR PLAYER: Shane Smeltz

PLAYERS TO WATCH:
Ryan Nelsen
Winston Reid
Chris Wood

FORMER STAR PLAYERS:
Wynton Rufer

TEAM NICKNAME:
The All Whites

In their first World Cup in Spain in 1982, New Zealand was in a difficult group with experienced opponents, including Brazil and Uruguay. New Zealand lost all three of their group matches and conceded a total of 12 goals.

Twenty-eight years later, New Zealand qualified for the 2010 World Cup in South Africa. This time New Zealand was unlucky to go home after the group stage. They didn't lose any of their three matches and earned a respectable 1–1 draw with Italy. The New Zealand team returned home with their pride intact.

▲ Chris Wood (right) of New Zealand shoots while Fabio Cannavaro of Italy tries to block the shot during the 2010 World Cup.

OTHER SPORTING SUCCESS

Football is not the primary sport for most New Zealanders. Rugby is more widely played, and the country has a long history of success in the sport. In 1987 New Zealand won the first ever Rugby World Cup, and repeated the success on home soil in 2011.

▲ The New Zealand rugby team celebrates after their victory against France in 2011.

DID YOU KNOW?

The New Zealand football team's nickname (the All Whites) is similar to the very famous nickname for their rugby team, who are known all over the world as the All Blacks.

NEW ZEALAND'S WORLD CUP RECORD	
PLAYED	6
WON	0
DRAWN	3
LOST	3
FOR	4
AGAINST	14
WIN %	0.0

Japan

CONTINENT: Asia
POPULATION: 126.5 million
CAPITAL CITY: Tokyo
CURRENCY: yen
LANGUAGE: Japanese
INTERNET: .jp
WORLD CUPS: 4
WORLD CUP WINS: 0
STAR PLAYER: Shinji Kagawa

PLAYERS TO WATCH:
Keisuke Honda

FORMER STAR PLAYERS:
Shinji Ono
Hidetoshi Nakata
Shunsuke Nakamura

TEAM NICKNAME:
Samurai Blue

Japan made their World Cup debut in France in 1998. Disappointingly for their fans, the team lost all three group matches and scored only one goal. Four years later Japan co-hosted the World Cup with South Korea. It was the first time that the tournament had been played in Asia and it was a great success. Japan drew their opening match and won the next two. Japan played Turkey in the second round and were beaten 1–0.

Japan had another disappointing World Cup in 2006 when the team was knocked out in the group stage. Four years later Japan beat Cameroon and Denmark to reach the second round for the second time in their history. Japan played well in a tight match against Paraguay. The match ended 0–0 after extra time, and Paraguay won in a penalty shoot-out.

SUMO

Football is not the most popular sport in Japan, where the national sport is Sumo – a type of wrestling (see above). There are no different weight classes in Sumo (as there are in boxing), and the wrestlers can be matched up against someone much bigger than themselves.

DID YOU KNOW?

Japan has an excellent women's football team. The team won the 2011 FIFA Women's World Cup and were runners-up at the 2012 Olympics.

JAPAN'S WORLD CUP RECORD	
PLAYED	14
WON	4
DRAWN	3
LOST	7
FOR	12
AGAINST	16
WIN %	28.57

The Republic of Korea
(South Korea)

CONTINENT: Asia

POPULATION: 48.4 million

CAPITAL CITY: Seoul

CURRENCY: won

LANGUAGE: Korean

INTERNET: .kr

WORLD CUPS: 8

WORLD CUP WINS: 0

STAR PLAYER: Sung-Yueng Ki

PLAYERS TO WATCH:
Park Chu-Young
Lee Chung-Yong

FORMER STAR PLAYERS:
Ahn Jung-Hwan

TEAM NICKNAME:
The Taeguk Warriors

South Korea played in the World Cup for the first time in 1954, in Switzerland. In two matches South Korea conceded a total of 16 goals and didn't score any goals themselves. It was 32 years before the country made it to the World Cup again, in 1986 in Mexico. Since then, South Korea has qualified for every World Cup tournament.

TOURNAMENT CO-HOSTS

South Korea co-hosted the 2002 FIFA World Cup with Japan. For the first time, the team made it all the way to the semi-final. After beating Portugal and Poland at the group stage, South Korea beat Italy in the second round. They then faced Spain in the quarter-final. The match ended 0–0 after extra time, and the Koreans held their nerve in the penalty shoot-out to win. In the semi-final, Germany beat the Koreans 1–0.

▲ South Korea striker Park Chu Young (right) heads the ball past Nigeria goalkeeper Vencent Enyeama during a World Cup match in 2010.

In 2006 South Korea was unable to proceed from their group at the World Cup. In the 2010 tournament in South Africa, South Korea made it into the second round but were beaten 2–1 by Ukraine.

SOUTH KOREA'S WORLD CUP RECORD	
PLAYED	28
WON	5
DRAWN	8
LOST	15
FOR	28
AGAINST	61
WIN %	17.85

DID YOU KNOW?

By reaching the semi-final in 2002, South Korea became the most successful team from Asia in World Cup history.

▼ Park Ji-Sung of South Korea (centre) is tackled by Michael Ballack of Germany during the 2002 World Cup semi-final.

EUROPE

Italy

CONTINENT: Europe
POPULATION: 60.8 million
CAPITAL CITY: Rome
CURRENCY: euro
LANGUAGE: Italian
INTERNET: .it
WORLD CUPS: 17
WORLD CUP WINS: 4 (1934, 1938, 1982, 2006)
STAR PLAYER: Mario Balotelli

PLAYERS TO WATCH:
Andrea Pirlo
Gianluigi Buffon
Daniele De Rossi

FORMER STAR PLAYERS:
Paolo Maldini
Roberto Baggio
Dino Zoff

TEAM NICKNAME:
La Squadra Azzura *or* Azzuri

Italy is the second most successful team in the history of the FIFA World Cup. The country has won the competition four times, and finished runners-up on two other occasions. Italy's most recent success at the World Cup came in 2006 in Germany (see captain Fabio Cannavaro, right). The team were not expected to do well at the tournament, but they defended extremely well and conceded only two goals in the entire competition. In the final, Italy drew with France 1–1 after extra time but went on to win the match in a penalty shoot-out.

▲ Italy's star player in 1994, Roberto Baggio, hits his penalty over the crossbar during the final penalty shoot-out.

WORLD CUP HOST COUNTRY

Italy has hosted the World Cup twice, in 1934 and 1990. Italy was victorious in 1934, beating Czechoslovakia in the final 2–1 after extra time. In 1990 Italy reached the semi-final but were beaten by Argentina. Italy managed to win the third place play-off match, beating England 2–1.

PENALTY HEARTBREAK

In 1994 Italy and Brazil reached the final of the World Cup in the United States. It was not an exciting match, and after extra time the score was level at 0–0. Three Italy players missed their penalties in the shoot-out to decide the match winner, as Brazil won 3–2. After playing so well throughout the competition, it was a heartbreaking result for the Italian players and their fans.

ITALY'S WORLD CUP RECORD	
PLAYED	80
WON	44
DRAWN	21
LOST	15
FOR	126
AGAINST	74
WIN %	55

Germany

CONTINENT: Europe
POPULATION: 82.1 million
CAPITAL CITY: Berlin
CURRENCY: euro
LANGUAGE: German
INTERNET: .de
WORLD CUPS: 17
WORLD CUP WINS
[AS WEST GERMANY]:
3 (1954, 1974, 1990)
STAR PLAYER: Mesut Özil

PLAYERS TO WATCH:
Thomas Müller
Philipp Lahm
Lukas Podolski
Mario Götze

FORMER STAR PLAYERS:
Franz Beckenbauer
Gerd Müller
Lothar Matthaeus

TEAM NICKNAME:
Die Mannschaft
or Nationalmannschaft

FOOTBALL FACTS

Germany has finished in third place at the last two World Cups, in 2006 and 2010.

Germany has played at 17 of the 19 World Cup tournaments. The German team has won the tournament three times (1954, 1974, and 1990) and hosted the competition twice: in 1974 and 2006. The German team won the tournament on home soil in 1974, beating the Netherlands 2–1 in the final. In 2006 they narrowly missed out on the final again, losing to Italy in the semi-final.

GERMANY'S WORLD CUP RECORD	
PLAYED	99
WON	60
DRAWN	19
LOST	20
FOR	207
AGAINST	117
WIN %	60.60

Germany has played in an incredible seven World Cup finals, and only Brazil can match this record. Germany has won the competition three times, but they have also been the runner-up on four other occasions (1966, 1982, 1986, and 2002).

2010 AWARDS

Thomas Müller, who was making his World Cup debut for Germany in 2010, ended the competition with two prestigious awards. He was named top scorer in the competition with five goals, and he received the FIFA Best Young Player award.

DID YOU KNOW?

Some of the players in the German national team, including Mesut Özil and Sami Khedira, have parents who were born in Turkey. Two other German stars, Lukas Podolski and Miroslav Klose, were both born in Poland.

The Netherlands

CONTINENT: Europe
POPULATION: 16.7 million
CAPITAL CITY: Amsterdam
CURRENCY: euro
LANGUAGE: Dutch
INTERNET: .nl
WORLD CUPS: 9
WORLD CUP WINS: 0
STAR PLAYER: Robin van Persie

PLAYERS TO WATCH:
Klass-Jan Huntelaar
Wesley Sneijder
Arjen Robben

FORMER STAR PLAYERS:
Johan Cruyff
Dennis Bergkamp
Marc Overmars

TEAM NICKNAME:
Oranje

The Netherlands was runner-up in the final of the 2010 World Cup, after a goal from Spain in the 116th minute of extra time made the score 1–0. After a successful tournament, and some very good performances up to that point, the Netherlands was disappointing in the final. Despite a couple of chances to score through their quick attacker Arjen Robben, the Netherlands was outplayed by a very good Spanish team. The 2010 final was a bad tempered match, and the Netherlands players received eight yellow cards and had one player sent off.

DID YOU KNOW?

Unlike a lot of other nations, football only became a professional sport in the Netherlands in the 1950s. Within two decades the Dutch national team had reached the final of the World Cup two times – an incredible achievement.

The 2010 World Cup final was the third time that the Dutch had been just 90 minutes away from winning the trophy. The team also made it to the final of the 1974 and 1978 World Cup tournaments. In 1974 they lost 2–1 to Germany, and in 1978 Argentina beat them 3–1. The Netherlands has the unenviable record of being the only team to have competed in three World Cup finals and to have lost them all.

THE NETHERLANDS' WORLD CUP RECORD	
PLAYED	43
WON	22
DRAWN	10
LOST	11
FOR	71
AGAINST	44
WIN %	51.16

▼ Rob Rensenbrink (right) of the Netherlands in a first round match at the 1974 World Cup.

Portugal

CONTINENT: Europe
POPULATION: 10.7 million
CAPITAL CITY: Lisbon
CURRENCY: euro
LANGUAGE: Portuguese
INTERNET: .pt
WORLD CUPS: 5
WORLD CUP WINS: 0
STAR PLAYER: Cristiano Ronaldo

PLAYERS TO WATCH:
Luis Nani
João Moutinho
Fàbio Coentrão

FORMER STAR PLAYERS:
Eusébio
Nuno Gomes

TEAM NICKNAME:
Selecção das Quinas

Portugal has had a good record for qualifying for the World Cup in recent times. The Portuguese team has played at the last three tournaments, but in the history of the competition they have only qualified for the World Cup five times. Portugal has reached the semi-final twice (in 1966 and 2006), and has only once failed to make it out of the group stage, in 1986.

GLORIOUS DEBUT

Portugal reached the semi-final of the World Cup when they made their debut in the 1966 competition in England. Eusébio scored 9 goals at the tournament, including an incredible four goals in the match against North Korea. Portugal met the host country in the semi-final, and lost 2–1. Portugal went on to win the third place play-off match against the Soviet Union. Eusébio was the top goalscorer at the 1966 World Cup.

▶ Eusébio (left) was awarded the Golden Shoe (now called the Golden Boot) for the nine goals he scored at the 1966 World Cup.

Portuguese football star Cristiano Ronaldo is one of the most famous and recognizable footballers in the world. In 2008 Ronaldo became the most expensive player in history when he transferred from Manchester United to Real Madrid for an £80 million fee.

PORTUGAL'S WORLD CUP RECORD	
PLAYED	23
WON	12
DRAWN	3
LOST	8
FOR	39
AGAINST	22
WIN %	52.17

England

CONTINENT: Europe
POPULATION: 53 million
CAPITAL CITY: London
CURRENCY: pound sterling
LANGUAGE: English
INTERNET: .uk
WORLD CUPS: 13
WORLD CUP WINS: 1
STAR PLAYER: Steven Gerrard

PLAYERS TO WATCH:
Alex Oxlade-Chamberlain
Joe Hart
Wayne Rooney

FORMER STAR PLAYERS:
Bobby Moore
Gary Lineker
David Beckham

TEAM NICKNAME:
The Three Lions

England is a regular participant in the World Cup, and many of the country's greatest-ever footballers have performed at the tournament. Stars such as Bobby Charlton (see below, centre) and Bobby Moore (see below, left) were integral members of the England team when it won its only World Cup, in 1966. Both players ended their careers with over 100 appearances for their country, and will always be remembered fondly for their part in England's greatest football success.

In recent World Cups the performance by the England team has struggled to match the expectation of the fans. England has qualified for the last four World Cups, but failed to get past the quarter-final stage. Overall the team has made only one semi-final appearance (in 1990) since they won the tournament in 1966.

ENGLAND'S WORLD CUP RECORD	
PLAYED	59
WON	26
DRAWN	19
LOST	14
FOR	77
AGAINST	52
WIN %	44.06

WORLD-FAMOUS PLAYER

David Beckham is one of the most recognizable sportspeople in the world. He is famous for his football skills and his lifestyle and was the centre of much attention during the 2002 World Cup held in South Korea and Japan. The Japanese fans (see above) were very excited by the England team's famous players, but mostly they wanted to catch a glimpse of Beckham and take his photograph or get his autograph.

France

CONTINENT: Europe
POPULATION: 63 million
CAPITAL CITY: Paris
CURRENCY: Euro
LANGUAGE: French
INTERNET: .fr
WORLD CUPS: 13
WORLD CUP WINS: 1
STAR PLAYER: Frank Ribery

PLAYERS TO WATCH:
Olivier Giroud
Karim Benzema
Yohan Cabaye

FORMER STAR PLAYERS:
Just Fontaine
Michel Platini
Zinedine Zidane

TEAM NICKNAME:
Les Bleus

France was one of the original 13 teams that took part in the first-ever World Cup tournament. France has also hosted the World Cup on two occasions: in 1938 and 1998. The country's first real success in the competition came in 1958 when they reached the semi-final and their striker Just Fontaine set the record for the most goals scored by one player at a World Cup competition.

GREAT TEAM – BUT UNLUCKY

In the 1980s France had a very good team, full of very talented players. On two occasions, in 1982 and 1986, the team reached the semi-final but they could not take the next step and reach their first final. In 1982 France was beaten in the semi-final by West Germany in one of the most thrilling matches in World Cup history. The match ended 1-1 after 90 minutes, but then 4 more goals were scored in extra time to leave the score at 3-3. A penalty shoot-out decided the winners.

▲ France's Michel Platini (seated) mourns as West German players celebrate victory in 1982.

HOME FAVOURITES

When France hosted the World Cup in 1998, their team was made up of players from a wide range of cultural backgrounds and ages – from teenagers to players in their 30s. The French team played extremely well in front of the passionate home crowds and managed to reach their first World Cup final. Their success over Brazil in the final match was followed by millions of people celebrating in the streets of the capital city Paris.

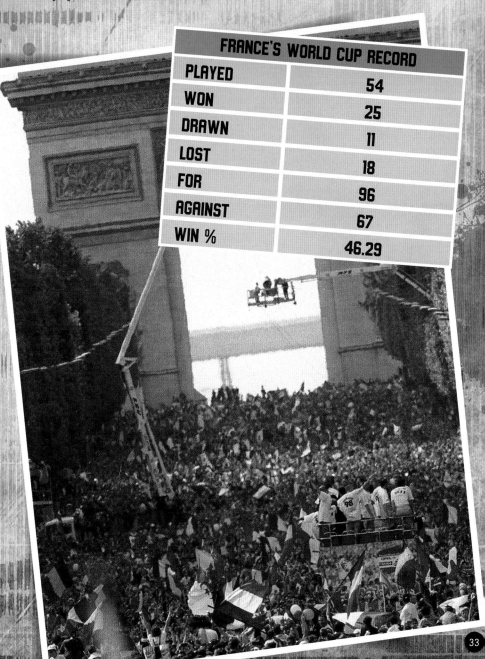

FRANCE'S WORLD CUP RECORD	
PLAYED	54
WON	25
DRAWN	11
LOST	18
FOR	96
AGAINST	67
WIN %	46.29

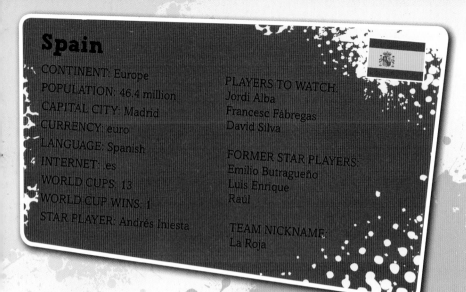

Spain

CONTINENT: Europe
POPULATION: 46.4 million
CAPITAL CITY: Madrid
CURRENCY: euro
LANGUAGE: Spanish
INTERNET: .es
WORLD CUPS: 13
WORLD CUP WINS: 1
STAR PLAYER: Andrés Iniesta

PLAYERS TO WATCH:
Jordi Alba
Francesc Fàbregas
David Silva

FORMER STAR PLAYERS:
Emilio Butragueño
Luis Enrique
Raúl

TEAM NICKNAME:
La Roja

In South Africa in 2010, after many appearances at the World Cup and some excellent performances by its teams over the years, Spain finally reached the final of the World Cup for the first time. Spain won by beating the Netherlands 1–0 in a tightly contested match.

TIKI-TAKA

The Spanish team (and their fans) have always been very proud of their football style. They like to pass the ball around and keep possession of it – a strategy that tires out their opponents and helps them to win matches. This style of football is known in Spain as *tiki-taka*. It takes many hours on the training pitch for the players to become comfortable and confident in this style of play. In recent years the Spanish team has been full of incredibly talented players who have mastered this style extremely well. As a result, the team has been very successful.

▼ Spain's Andrés Iniesta scores the winning goal in the 2010 World Cup final against the Netherlands.

SPAIN'S WORLD CUP RECORD	
PLAYED	56
WON	28
DRAWN	12
LOST	16
FOR	88
AGAINST	59
WIN %	50

NORTH AMERICA

Mexico

CONTINENT: North America
POPULATION: 114.8 million
CAPITAL CITY: Mexico City
CURRENCY: peso
LANGUAGE: Spanish
Internet: .mx
WORLD CUPS: 14
WORLD CUP WINS: 0
STAR PLAYER: Javier Hernández

PLAYERS TO WATCH:
Andrés Guardado
Giovani Dos Santos

FORMER STAR PLAYERS:
Hugo Sánchez
Cuauhtémoc Blanco

TEAM NICKNAME:
El Tri

Mexico has a good record of qualifying for the World Cup, and has participated in the last five tournaments. The 2014 tournament will be the country's 15th appearance, and only Brazil, Argentina, Italy, and Germany have appeared more times. Mexico's best result at the World Cup came in 1970 when they reached the quarter-final but lost against the eventual finalists, Italy.

TWO-TIME HOSTS

Mexico is one of a handful of countries, including France and Germany, to be chosen to host the World Cup on more than one occasion. Mexico was the World Cup host nation in 1970, when the tournament was an opportunity for Mexico to show the rest of the world its culture, colours, sounds – and some incredible football! The 1970 World Cup final between Brazil and Italy is regarded as one of the greatest football matches in history.

Mexico was again chosen as host nation for the 1986 World Cup. The tournament was originally supposed to be held in Colombia, but FIFA was uncertain that the country could stage an international football tournament satisfactorily. Mexico showed itself more prepared than many other nations to swiftly rise to the challenge of hosting the tournament again.

BRIGHT FUTURE?

The future of Mexican football looks very bright indeed! The team is full of young, dynamic, attacking footballers that have played together in youth teams and at other FIFA tournaments for many years. In 2012 a young Mexican team beat Brazil in the final of the Olympic football tournament to win the gold medal (see below).

MEXICO'S WORLD CUP RECORD	
PLAYED	49
WON	12
DRAWN	13
LOST	24
FOR	52
AGAINST	89
WIN %	24.48

United States of America

CONTINENT: North America
POPULATION: 313 million
CAPITAL CITY: Washington D.C.
CURRENCY: US dollar
LANGUAGE: English
INTERNET: .us
WORLD CUPS: 9
WORLD CUP WINS: 0
STAR PLAYER: Landon Donovan

PLAYERS TO WATCH:
Michael Bradley
Clint Dempsey
Tim Howard

FORMER STAR PLAYERS:
Eric Wynalda
Kasey Keller
Alexi Lalas

TEAM NICKNAME:
Stars and Stripes

DID YOU KNOW?

Football, or *soccer* as it is known in the United States, is very popular – but not as popular as traditional American sports such as baseball, American football, and basketball.

The United States played at three of the first four World Cup tournaments up until 1950 and finished in third place at the inaugural competition in 1930. After such a promising start, the United States failed to qualify for the World Cup again until 1990.

▼ Shock result! The United States beat England 2-1 at the 1950 World Cup.

HOSTING THE TOURNAMENT

In 1994 the United States was chosen by FIFA to be the host country for the World Cup. It was the first time the competition had been played in the United States. It was a success, with packed stadiums full of enthusiastic fans and some great football played by the competing teams. Since hosting the World Cup in 1994, the United States has not failed to qualify for the prestigious tournament, and the team has regularly made it through the group stage. The best finish by the United States at the World Cup was in 2002 when they reached the quarter-final.

FOOTBALL FACTS

The most famous and recognizable United States footballer is Landon Donovan (see above, left). He has played at three World Cups and was named FIFA Best Young Player for his performances at the tournament in 2002.

UNITED STATES WORLD CUP RECORD	
PLAYED	29
WON	7
DRAWN	5
LOST	17
FOR	32
AGAINST	56
WIN %	24.13

Ghana

CONTINENT: Africa
POPULATION: 25 million
CAPITAL CITY: Accra
CURRENCY: cedi
LANGUAGE: English, Akan, Ewe
INTERNET: .gh
WORLD CUPS: 2
WORLD CUP WINS: 0
STAR PLAYER: Asamoah Gyan

PLAYERS TO WATCH:
Michael Essien
Sulley Ali Muntari
Jordan Ayew
Kevin Prince-Boateng

FORMER STAR PLAYERS:
Abédi Pelé
Tony Yeboah

TEAM NICKNAME:
The Black Stars

Ghana is a relative newcomer to the World Cup, and they have only made two appearances at the tournament so far (in 2006 and 2010). At the 2006 World Cup in Germany, the young Ghana team made its debut in the competition and surprised many with their tremendous skill, determination, and togetherness. The team succeeded where other more experienced African nations failed by reaching the second round of the competition.

CRUEL EXIT

Ghana followed up their encouraging performance at the 2006 World Cup by qualifying again in 2010. This time they played even better and reached the quarter-final, becoming only the second team from Africa in World Cup history to reach that stage. After beating the United States in a very close match, Ghana played Uruguay in the quarter-final. Ghana exited the competition after Asamoah Gyan missed a penalty near the end of the match that would have given them victory. Uruguay won the match after a penalty shoot-out and Ghana was out of the competition. The team and their fans could be very proud of their performance.

THE ONES TO WATCH?

Ghana won the FIFA Under-20s World Cup in 2009 for the first time. Players who starred in that exciting team are now playing for the senior national team. The future looks bright for Ghana, and the team will be expecting to add to their two appearances at the world's premier football tournament.

GHANA'S WORLD CUP RECORD	
PLAYED	9
WON	4
DRAWN	2
LOST	3
FOR	9
AGAINST	10
WIN %	44.44

Nigeria

CONTINENT: Africa

POPULATION: 162.4 million

CAPITAL CITY: Lagos

CURRENCY: naira

LANGUAGE: English, Yoruba, Ibo, Hausa

INTERNET: .ng

WORLD CUPS: 4

WORLD CUP WINS: 0

STAR PLAYER: Peter Odemwingie

PLAYERS TO WATCH:
Vincent Enyeama
John Obi Mikel
Victor Moses

FORMER STAR PLAYERS:
Jay Jay Okocha
Nwankwo Kanu
Finidi George

TEAM NICKNAME:
The Super Eagles

Nigeria qualified for the World Cup for the first time in 1994, when the competition was held in the United States. The team enjoyed a fantastic debut, winning two matches in the group stage to proceed to the second round. They were knocked out of the tournament by Italy, 2–1, but the Nigeria team had represented Africa well and their fans could be proud of their achievement.

▼ In two out of four World Cup tournaments Nigeria has been placed in a group with Argentina and Greece (in 1994 and 2010).

After the 1994 finals, Nigeria qualified for the next two tournaments. They topped their group and entered the second round in 1998, but failed to repeat this in 2002. In 2010 Nigeria managed to qualify for the World Cup for the fourth time in their history. Vincent Enyeama, Nigeria's goalkeeper, put in a very good performance against Argentina, but they lost the match 1–0. After another draw and a defeat against Greece, they exited the competition.

NIGERIA'S WORLD CUP RECORD

PLAYED	14
WON	4
DRAWN	2
LOST	8
FOR	17
AGAINST	21
WIN %	28.57

WORLD CUP HEROICS

The Nigerian team that played at the 1994 World Cup will always be fondly remembered by football fans. There were some great players and they all appeared to be enjoying the experience of performing on football's biggest stage. The Nigeria team was always exciting to watch.

FOOTBALL FACTS

Nigeria won the football tournament at the 1996 Olympics in the United States.

GLOSSARY

altitude height of something above sea level

autograph signature of a famous person

co-host jointly host an event. For example, Japan and South Korea co-hosted the 2002 World Cup.

concede fail to prevent an opponent scoring

cricket sport played outdoors by two teams with a bat, a ball, and two wickets

Cricket World Cup international cricket tournament

Czechoslovakia country in Eastern Europe that separated into Slovakia and the Czech Republic in 1993

debut someone making their first appearance. For example, a footballer playing at the World Cup for the first time is making their debut.

extra time extra period of play that is added to a football match if it is a draw at the end of regulation time (90 minutes). Extra time lasts for 30 minutes, with two halves of 15 minutes each.

Fédération Internationale de Football Association (FIFA) international organization responsible for football around the world

FIFA Best Young Player award award given to the young player who has performed best at the World Cup

goal difference difference between the goals scored and conceded by a team. If a team has scored 1 goal and conceded 2, then the team has a goal difference of -1.

handball foul committed during a match when a player touches the football with their hand

inaugural marking or celebrating the beginning of something

integral essential part of something

Olympics international athletic competition held every four years

penalty shoot-out after extra time, if the score is still level, the two teams pick five players to try to score five penalties. The team that scores the most penalties wins.

prestigious something that is very important or special

rugby sport using an oval ball that players can kick or carry

Rugby World Cup international rugby tournament

send off when a referee shows a red card to a player either for a serious foul or for two yellow cards. The player has to leave the field of play.

Soviet Union former union of Eastern European countries, including Russia, which broke up in 1991

West Germany between 1945 and 1990 Germany was split into two countries: West Germany and East Germany

yellow card caution given to a player when they commit a foul or engage in unsporting behaviour

FIND OUT MORE

BOOKS

A–Z of the World Cup (World Cup Fever), Michael Hurley (Raintree, 2014)

Defender (Football Files), Michael Hurley (Raintree, 2011)

Fantastic Football, Clive Gifford (Oxford University Press, 2010)

Goalkeeper (Football Files), Michael Hurley (Raintree, 2011)

Midfielder (Football Files), Michael Hurley (Raintree, 2011)

Soccer (DK: Eyewitness Books), Hugh Hornby (DK Publishing, 2010)

Steven Gerrard (World Cup Heroes), Adam Cottier (John Blake Publishing, 2010

Striker (Football Files), Michael Hurley (Raintree, 2011)

The Kingfisher Football Encyclopaedia, Clive Gifford (Kingfisher, 2010)

Wayne Rooney (World Cup Heroes), Adam Cottier (John Blake Publishing, 2010

World Cup 2014 (World Cup Fever), Michael Hurley (Raintree, 2014)

World Cup Heroes (World Cup Fever), Michael Hurley (Raintree, 2014)

WEBSITES

www.fifa.com
The official website for everything World Cup related. You can find the latest team and player news, fixtures, results, and photos.

www.fifa.com/worldcup/archive/index.html
This is a great place to start if you want to find out facts and stats from previous World Cups. You can find stats from every match played and goals scored at all of the World Cup tournaments.

www.footballworldcupbrazil2014.com
This unofficial guide to the 2014 World Cup provides videos, blogs, team profiles, and facts and figures about previous World Cup tournaments.

kids.nationalgeographic.co.uk/kids/places/find/brazil
If you want to know more about Brazil, the host of the 2014 World Cup, and the history, geography, and culture of the country, this is a great place to start.

www.goal.com/en-gb/news/3841/world-cup-2014
Check out this website for the latest news on the teams battling to qualify for the World Cup.

news.bbc.co.uk/1/hi/world/americas/country_ profiles/1227110.stm
Find up-to-date news and information about Brazil's history, geography, politics, and economy.

LOOK IT UP...

1. Most international teams have a nickname. For example, the England team is known as "The Three Lions" because there are three lions on England's team badge. Do you know or can you find out which teams the following nicknames belong to?

   Les Éléphants   The Reggae Boyz

   White Eagles   Bafana Bafana

   Desert Foxes   Tricolorii

   The Pharaohs   The Zebras

2. Only two countries have ever retained the World Cup, which means that they won two tournaments in a row. Do you know or can you find out which countries have achieved this feat?

INDEX